CONTENTS

MEET THE MINIATURE HORSE

Have you ever heard of the miniature horse? The word "miniature" means small.

Miniature horses come in all the same colors that full-sized horses do. Here you can see a field with many American miniature horses.

Miniature horses are not baby horses. They are not ponies, either. Miniature horses are horses that have been **bred** to be small.

Here two American miniature horses jump over a small stone wall. Miniature horses like to run and jump, just as their full-sized relatives do.

There are rules that a horse must meet to be called a miniature horse. A miniature horse must be less than 34 to 38 inches (86–96 cm) at the lowest hairs of its mane.

Miniature horses are bred for many uses. One of these uses is as a family pet. They can live inside people's homes, as pet dogs do.

A big field for running and eating will make any horse happy, including a miniature horse.

Miniature horses need time outside, too. In fact, they will be much happier as outdoor pets. They just need a small

Do you live in a place that is warm most of the year? If so, a place with a roof where your horses can get out of the Sun is a good idea.

barn to sleep inside and to protect them from the weather. They also need a fenced area where they can run and **graze**.

Some miniature horses are trained for a special job. These special minis are guide horses for the blind.

Even miniature horses that do not end up becoming guide horses can make great pets. A calm, friendly horse can be a great pet for children.

Not every miniature horse is right for this job. It takes lots of training and tests to make sure the horse is smart and calm enough to be a guide. The horses that are able help blind people live more

This girl has a Shetland pony. Shetland ponies are bigger than miniature horses and smaller than full-size horses.

independent lives. The horses that do not become guide horses are **adopted** by families who want a well-trained pet.

A horse's gait is the way it moves. The miniature horse has four natural gaits: the walk, the trot, the canter, and the gallop.

Miniature horses are not big enough for people to ride safely. They can pull people in carts or wagons, though.

This is a Falabella miniature horse. This is one of the smallest kinds of mini horse.

Most miniature horses are strong enough to pull two grown-ups in a cart.

Some people like to show their miniature horses. In one kind of show, judges **compare** miniature horses to each other and decide which one is closest to the standard.

This miniature horse is grazing. Grazing is the act of eating grass.

11

MINI HORSE CARE

Miniature horses like to be **groomed**. They should be brushed every day. They will also shed their hair twice a year.

This miniature horse had some special grooming. Her owner braided her mane and tied it with a ribbon!

This means old hair falls out so new hair can grow. Extra brushing at these times is a good idea.

Grooming your miniature horse can be a great time to connect with your pet. You need to brush its coat and mane and clean its hooves.

Your mini horse may need to be bathed sometimes. Too many baths dries out their skin, though. Outdoor baths are the safest and easiest way to go.

Just as with dogs and cats, mini horses should see the vet at least once a year. They will get a checkup and shots to keep them healthy.

These are some of the tools a farrier uses to work on horses' hooves. Farriers clean and trim the hooves, but they also check for any problems.

Horses also need to have their hooves clipped every 6 to 8 weeks. The person who trims a horse's hooves is called a farrier.

A farrier can also fit your miniature
horse with shoes. Horseshoes will
protect your horse's feet.

MINI HORSE DIET

Every pet needs the right food. Miniature horses are no different. Grasses and grains are the natural foods for a mini horse.

This miniature horse has a dappled, or spotted, coat.

Mini horses can be fed hay when there is no grass. Horses also need salt and **trace minerals**. These are sold in

Your miniature horse will like eating fresh grass. However, you should make sure your pet does not eat too much.

bricks. Small amounts of apples and carrots can be given to mini horses as a sweet treat. Clean, cool water should always be out for your mini horse, too.

Miniature horses are known for overeating. A heavy horse is an unhealthy horse. A miniature horse that is overweight can have problems with its feet. It can have other health problems, too.

You can feed your horse treats, but do not give it too much of these foods. Use small amounts of special foods for training.

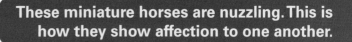

It is important to give your horse healthy foods. You need to watch your horse to make sure it is not grazing too much. You also need to be sure you are not giving it too many treats.

A miniature horse can be a great pet for your family. These horses live for about 20 years.

This means they can become a real part of your family. However, it also means they will be a lot of responsibility for a long time.

Owning any pet is a big decision. Only take in a miniature horse or other pet if you know you can take care of it. You may end up with a really fun and rewarding pet!

GUESS WHAT?

You need to be careful that your miniature horse does not graze too much when the grass is long. This can cause founder, which is a very painful illness.

Some miniature horses are even smaller than regular ones. Miniature horses are sometime born with dwarfism. Dwarfism is a condition that causes small size, among other things.

The American Miniature Horse Association (AMHA) says a horse can only be called a miniature horse if it is under 34 inches (86 cm).

One bale of hay is enough food for a miniature horse for one week.

Horses, including miniature horses, have teeth that keep growing throughout their lives. It is possible to find out about how old a horse is by looking at its teeth.

GLOSSARY

ADOPTED (uh-DOPT-ed) To take something for your own or as your own choice.

BRED (BRED) To have brought a male and a female animal together so they will have babies.

COMPARE (kum-PAYR) To see how two or more things are alike or different.

GRAZE (GRAYZ) To feed on grass.

GROOMED (GROOMD) Cleaned someone's body and make it neat.

INDEPENDENT (in-dih-PEN-dent) Free from the control of others.

TRACE MINERALS (trays MIN-eh-rulz) Small amounts of hard, natural matter that comes from the ground.

READ MORE

Hansen, Rosanna. *Panda: A Guide Horse for Ann*. Honesdale, PA: Boyds Mills Press, 2005.

Hudak, Heather. Thumbelina: *The World's Smallest Horse*. New York: Weigl Publishers, 2008.

Lunis, Natalie. *Miniature Horses*. New York: Bearport Publishing, 2009.

INDEX

WEB SITES

For Web resources related to the subject of this book, go to: www.windmillbooks.com/weblinks and select this book's title.

CURIOUS PET PALS

MY FRIEND THE MINIATURE HORSE

JOANNE RANDOLPH

WINDMILL
BOOKS
New York

Published in 2011 by Windmill Books, LLC
303 Park Avenue South, Suite # 1280, New York, NY 10010-3657

First Edition

Editor: Jennifer Way
Book Design: Erica Clendening
Layout Design: Julio Gil
Photo Researcher: Jessica Gerweck

Photo Credits: Cover, pp. 4, 5, 6, 7, 9 (top, bottom), 11 (top, bottom), 12, 13, 14, 15, 16, 17 Shutterstock.com; p. 8 © www.iStockphoto.com/Karen Wunderman; p. 10 © www.iStockphoto.com/Michelle Harvey; p. 18 © www.iStockphoto.com/Trevor Hunt; p. 19 © www.iStockphoto.com/Janet Hill; p. 20 © www.iStockphoto.com/Thomas Rubin; p. 21 © Juniors Bildarchiv/age fotostock.

Library of Congress Cataloging-in-Publication Data

Randolph, Joanne.
 My friend the miniature horse / by Joanne Randolph.
    p. cm. — (Curious pet pals)
 Includes index.
 ISBN 978-1-60754-976-5 (library binding) — ISBN 978-1-60754-984-0 (pbk.) — ISBN 978-1-61533-111-6 (6-pack)
 1. Miniature horses—Juvenile literature. I. Title.
 SF293.M56R36 2011
 636.1—dc22
                                                2010004695

Manufactured in the United States of America

For more great fiction and nonfiction, go to www.windmillbooks.com.

CPSIA Compliance Information: Batch #BW2011WM: For Further Information contact Windmill Books, New York, New York at 1-866-478-0556